Intermediate to Late Intermediate

AT THE MOVIES

BOOK 3

DAN COATES

POPULAR PIANO LIBRARY

CONTENTS

Adelieland 2

As Time Goes By 5

Can You Read My Mind? 8

The Colors of the Wind 11

Fame 16

Into the West. 20

The Pink Panther 29

A Whole New World. 26

Produced by
Alfred Music Publishing Co., Inc.
P.O. Box 10003
Van Nuys, CA 91410-0003
alfred.com

Printed in USA.

ISBN-10: 0-7390-7516-0
ISBN-13: 978-0-7390-7516-6

ADELIELAND
Happy Feet

By John Powell
Arranged by Dan Coates

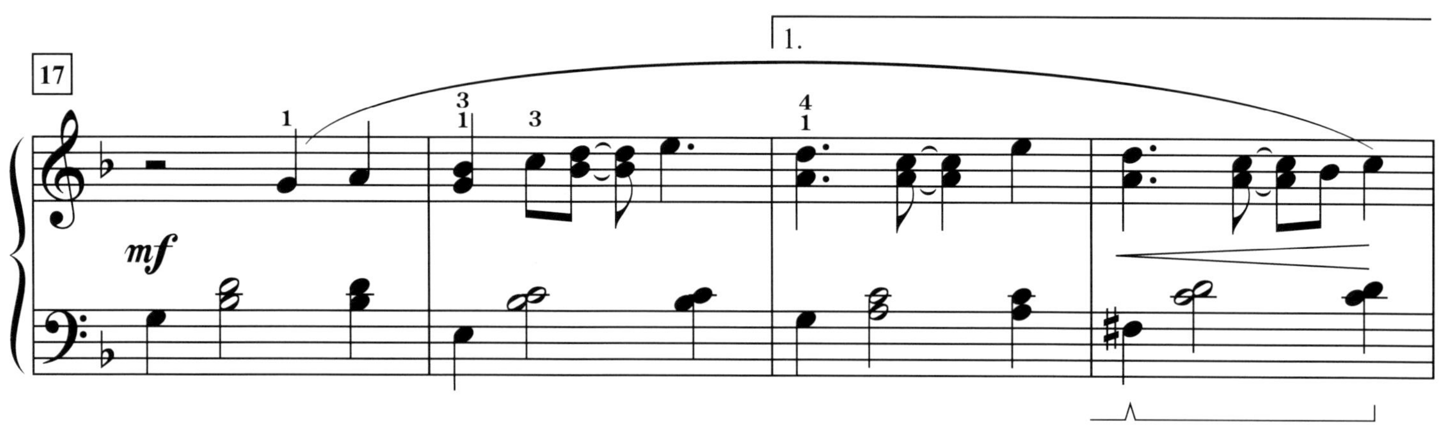

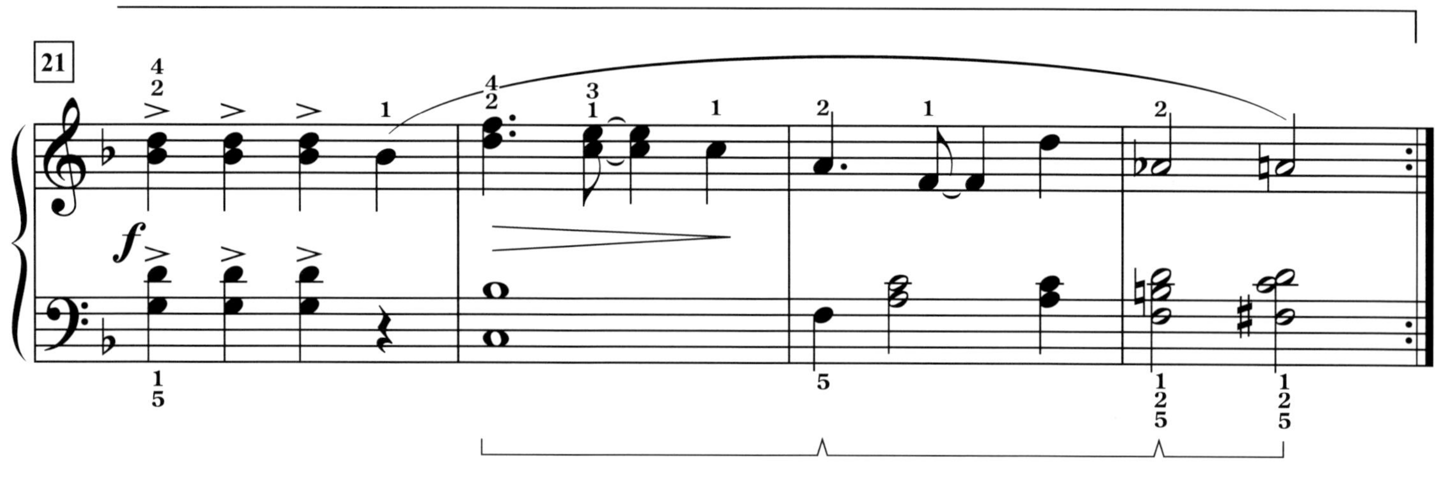

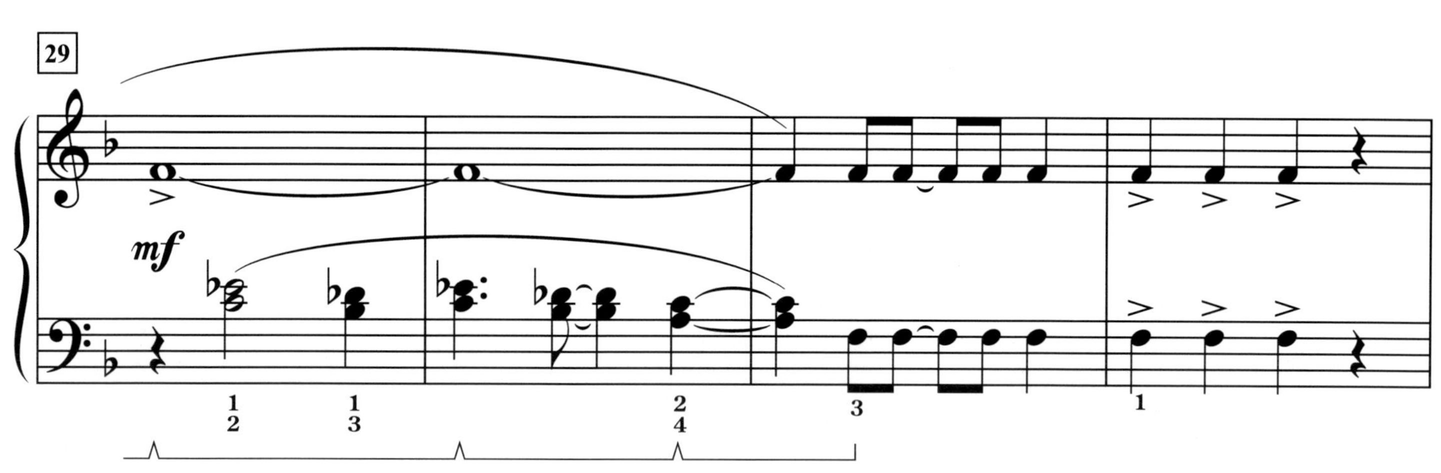

4
33
cresc.
f
37
mf
41
ff
45
f
49
ff

AS TIME GOES BY
Casablanca

Words and Music by Herman Hupfeld
Arranged by Dan Coates

11
when two lov - ers woo,   they   still say, "I love you,"   on   that you can   re - ly;
14
no   mat - ter what the   fu - ture   brings, as   time   goes
17
by.   Moon-light   and love songs
mf
20
nev - er out of date,   hearts full   of pas - sion,   jeal - ou - sy and hate;

wom - an needs man and man must have his mate; that no one can de -
ny. It's still the same old sto - ry, a fight for love and glo - ry, a
case of do or die! The world will al - ways wel - come
lov - ers, as time goes by. You by.

CAN YOU READ MY MIND?
Superman

Words by Leslie Bricusse
Music by JOHN WILLIAMS
Arranged by Dan Coates

look at me quiv-er-ing like a lit-tle girl shiv-er-ing. You can
see right through me. Can you read my
mind? Can you pic-ture the things I'm think-ing of?
Won-d'ring why you are all the won-der-ful things you

24
are. You can fly. You be-long to the sky. You and
mf
27
I could be-long to each oth - er. If you need a
mf
30
friend, I'm the one to fly to. If you
31
mf
33
need to be loved, here I am. Read my mind!
mf

THE COLORS OF THE WIND
Pocahontas

Lyrics by Stephen Schwartz
Music by Alan Menken
Arranged by Dan Coates

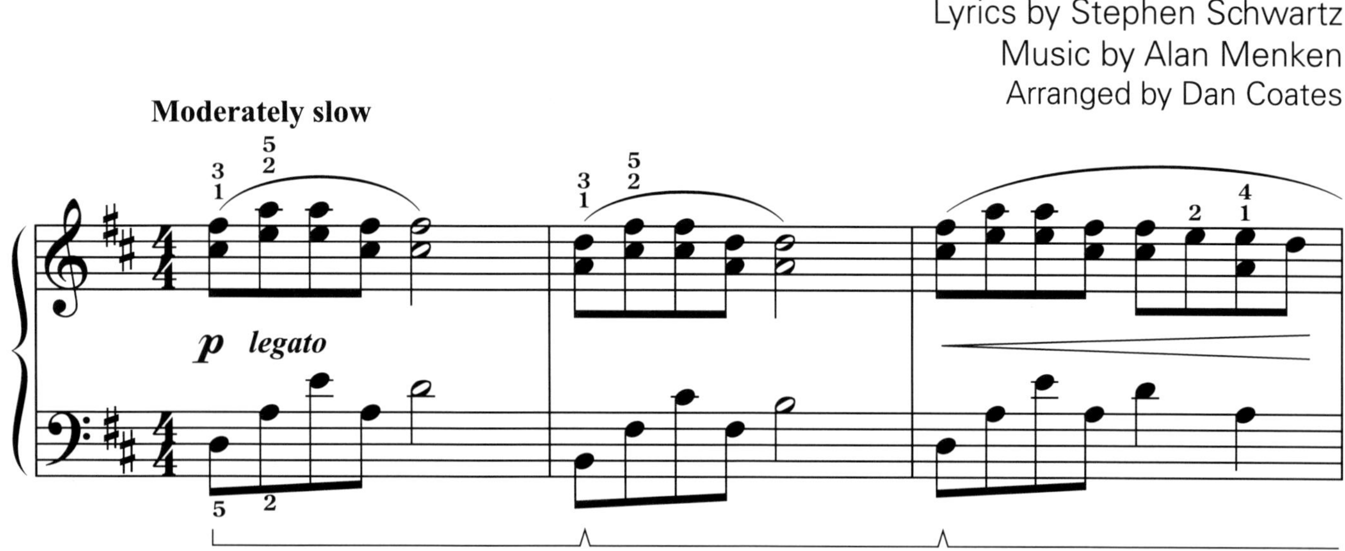

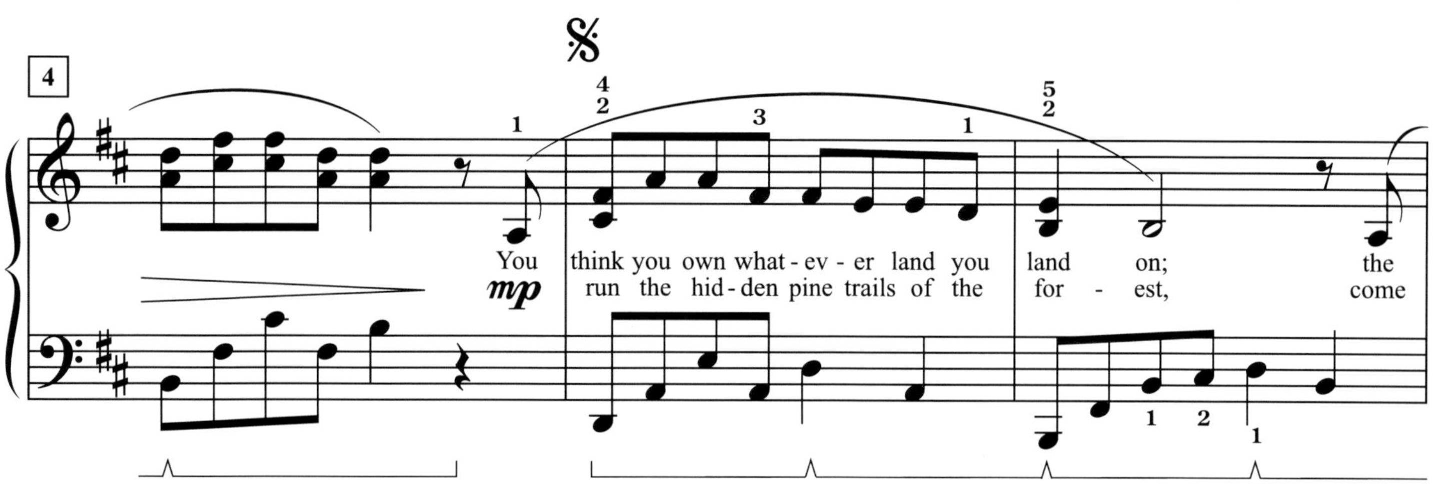

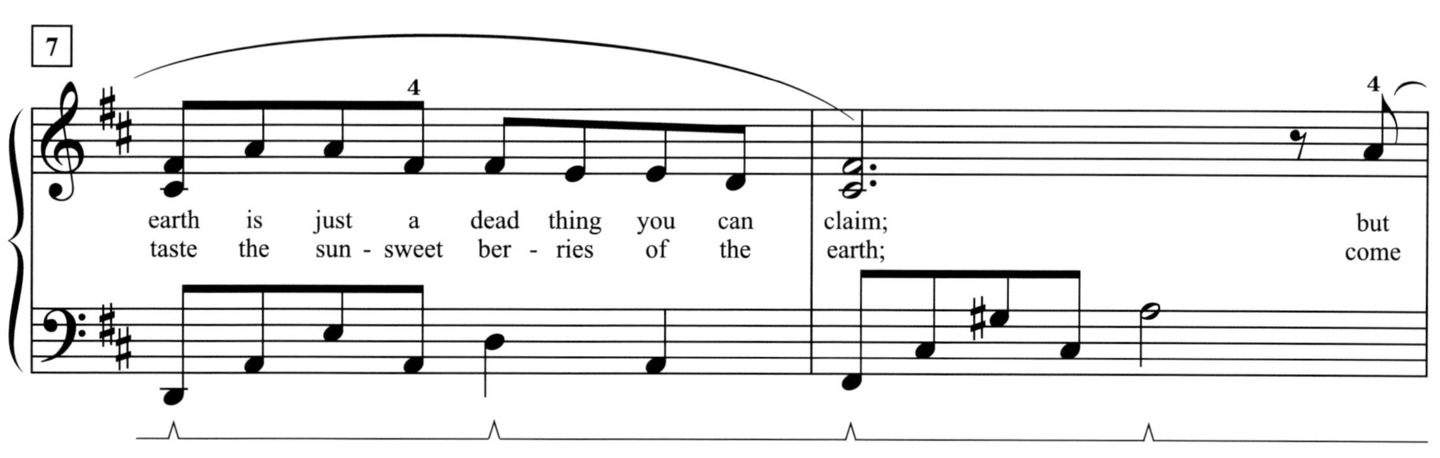

9
I know ev - 'ry rock and tree and crea - ture has a life, has a spi - rit, has a
roll in all the rich - es all a - round you, and for once, nev - er won - der what they're
12
name.
worth.
You think the on - ly peo - ple who are peo - ple are the
The rain - storm and the riv - er are my broth - ers; the
15
peo - ple who look and think like you, but
her - on and the ot - ter are my friends; and
to Coda
17
if you walk the foot - steps of a stran - ger you'll learn things you nev - er knew you nev - er
we are all con - nect - ed to each oth - er in a cir - cle, in a hoop that nev - er

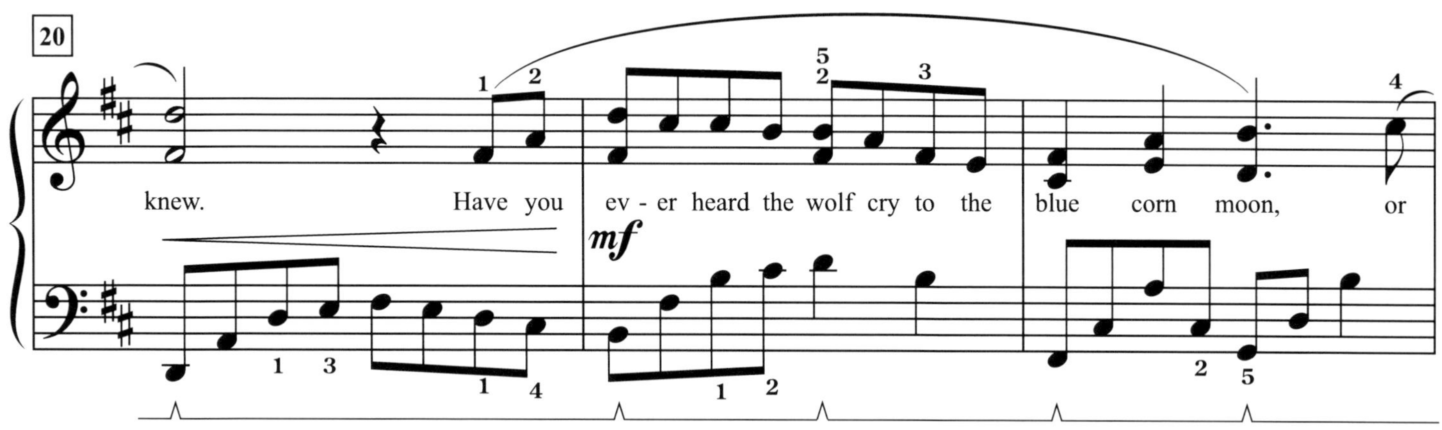
20
mf
knew. Have you ev - er heard the wolf cry to the blue corn moon, or

23
asked the grin - ning bob - cat why he grinned? Can you

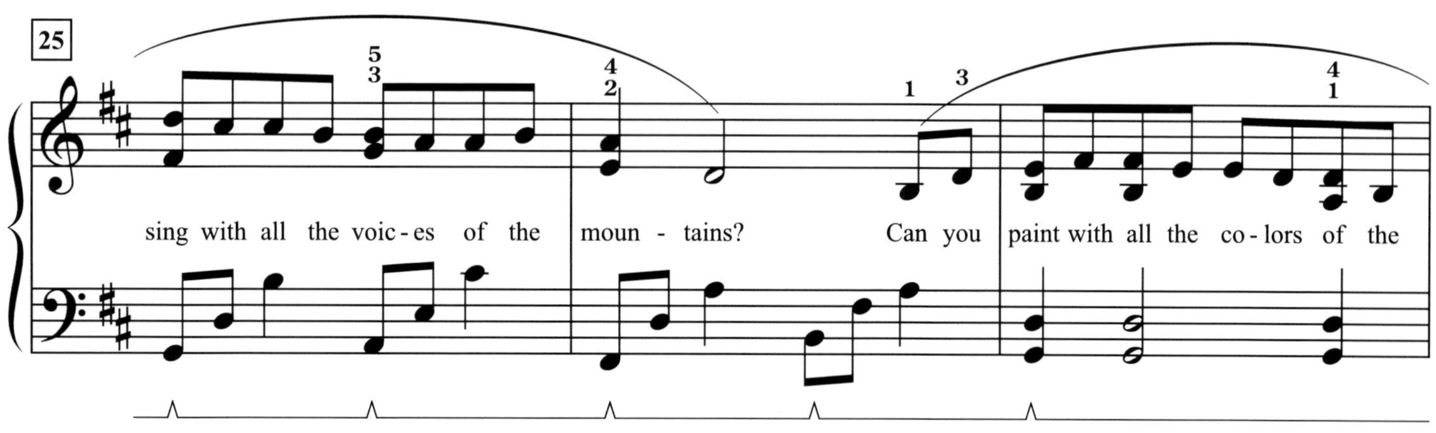
25
sing with all the voic - es of the moun - tains? Can you paint with all the co - lors of the

28
wind? Can you paint with all the co - lors of the wind?

31
D.S. al Coda
Come
Coda
ends.
mf
How high will the syc-a-more grow? If you
37
rit.
cut it down, then you'll nev - er know.
And you'll
a tempo
40
f
nev - er hear the wolf cry to the blue corn moon, for whe-ther we are white or cop-per

43
skinned,   we need to   sing with all the voic-es of the   moun - tains,   need to

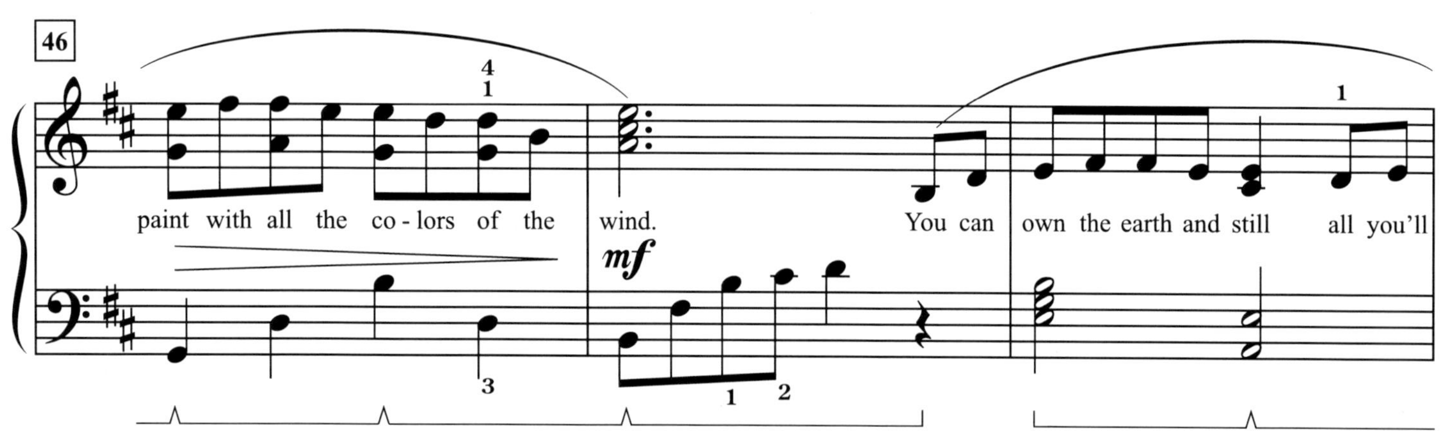
46
paint with all the co - lors of the   wind.   mf   You can own the earth and still   all you'll

49
a tempo
own is earth un - til   you can paint with all the co - lors of the   wind.
rit.

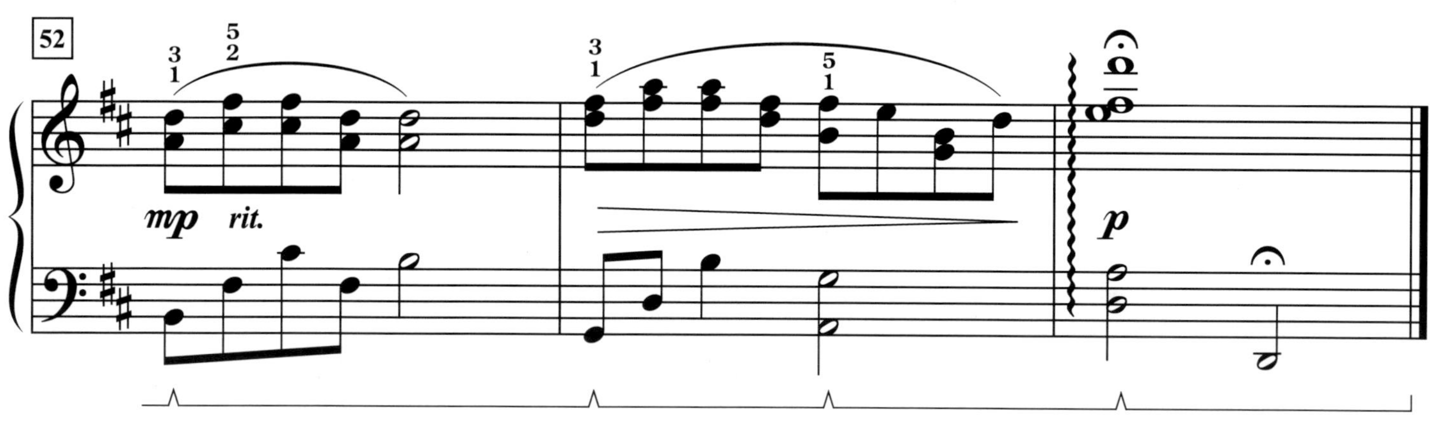
52
mp rit.
p

FAME
Fame

Moderately fast
Re - mem - ber, re - mem - ber, re - mem - ber, re - mem - ber, re - mem - ber, re - mem - ber,
re - mem - ber, re - mem - ber. Re - mem - ber, re - mem - ber, re - mem - ber, re - mem - ber,
re - mem - ber, re - mem - ber, re - mem - ber, re - mem - ber.
1. Ba - by,
2. Ba - by,
look at me, and tell me what you see.
hold me tight, 'cause you can make it right.

You ain't seen the best of me yet.
You can shoot me straight to the top.
Give me time, I'll make
you for - get the rest.
all I got to give.
I got more in me,
Ba - by, I'll be tough,
and you can set it free.
too much is not e - nough.
I can catch the moon
I can ride your heart
in my hand.
'til it breaks.
Don't you know who I am?
Ooh, I got what it takes.
Re - mem - ber my

25
f
name. Fame!
I'm gon-na live for-ev - er.
I'm gon-na learn how to

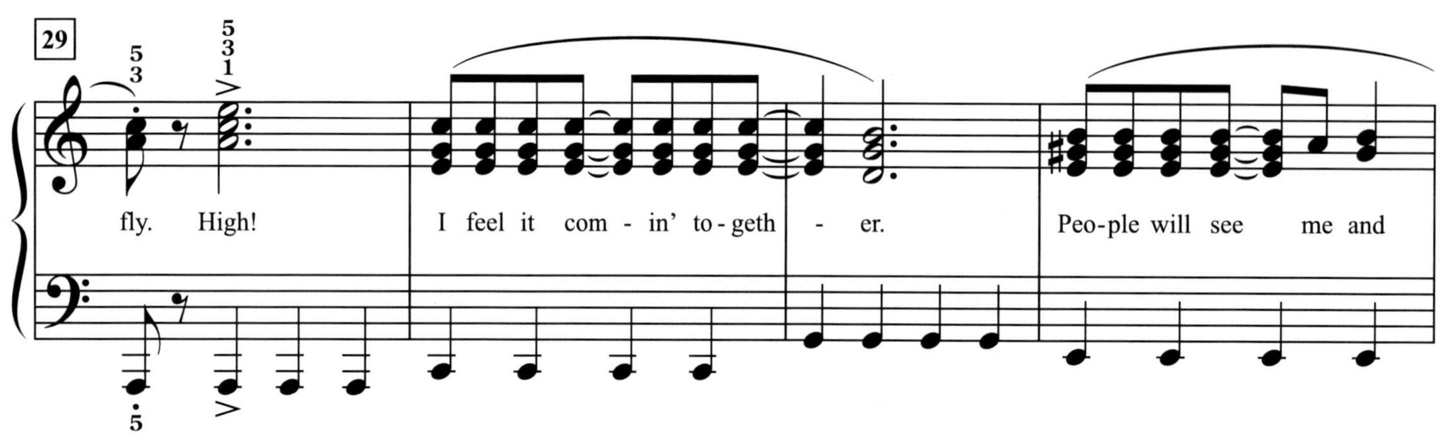
29
fly. High!
I feel it com - in' to-geth - er.
Peo-ple will see me and

33
die. Fame!
I'm gon-na make it to heav - en.
Light up the sky like a

37
flame. Fame!
I'm gon-na live for-ev - er.
Ba - by, rem - mem - ber my

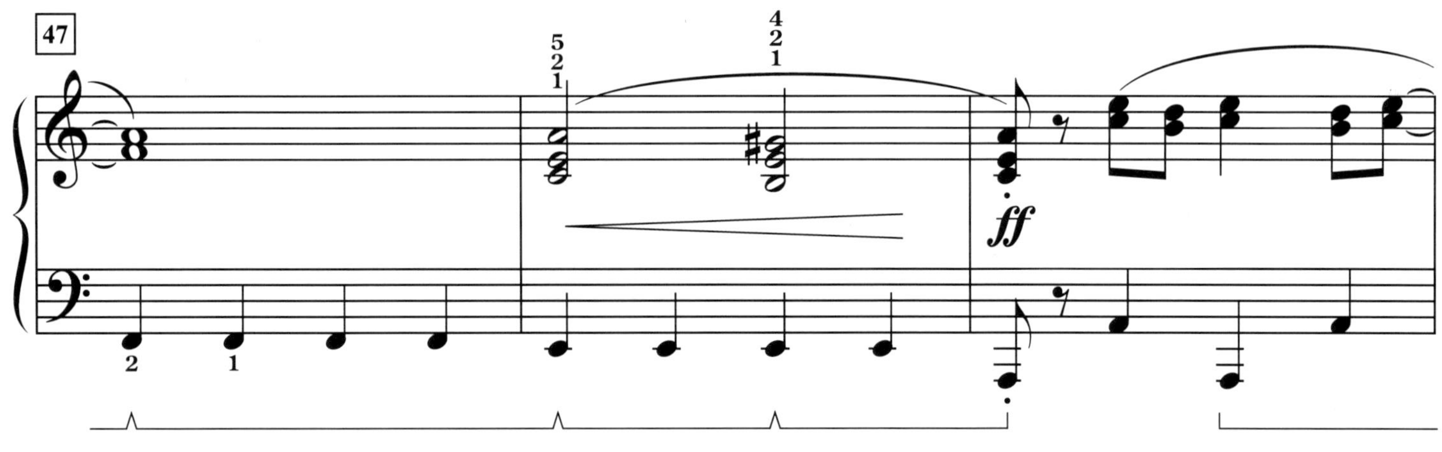
41
mf
8va
name. Re - mem - ber,   re - mem - ber,   re - mem - ber,   re - mem - ber,   re - mem - ber,   re - mem - ber,
44
re - mem - ber,   re - mem - ber.
f

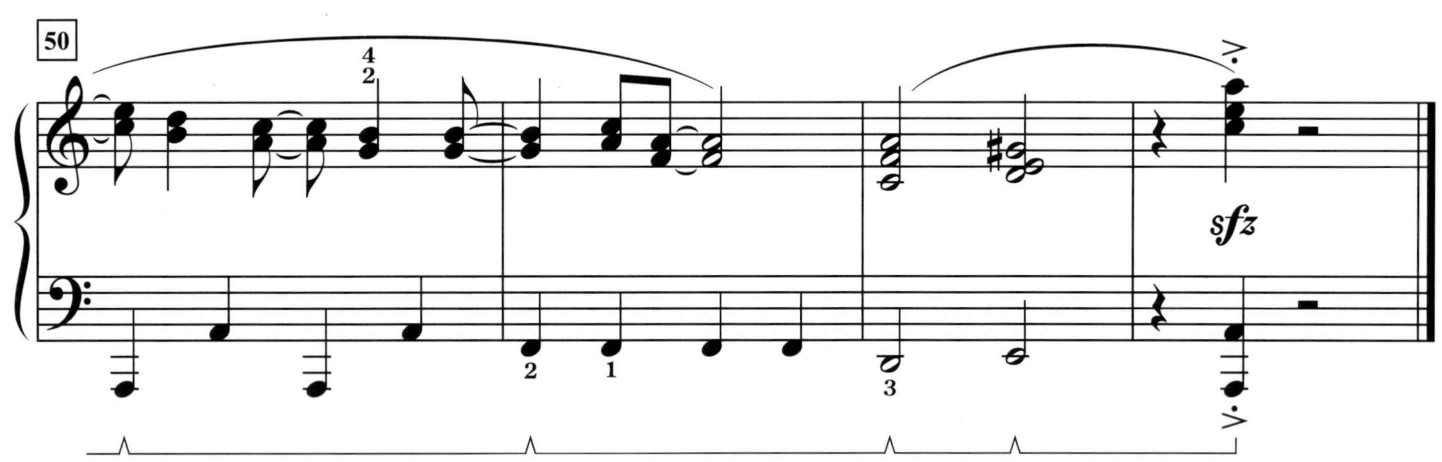
47
ff
50
sfz

INTO THE WEST
Lord of the Rings: The Return of the King

Words and Music by
Howard Shore, Fran Walsh and Annie Lennox
Arranged by Dan Coates

14
3
4
now.
Dream
of the ones who came be - fore.
17
3
1 2
They are call - ing
from a-cross the dis - tant
20
3
shore.
mp
Why do you weep?
23
What are these tears
up - on   your face?
Soon you will see
5

26
all of your fears will pass a-way.
29
cresc.
Safe in my arms, you're on-ly sleep - ing.
33
f
What can you see on the ho - ri - zon?
37
Why do the white gulls call?

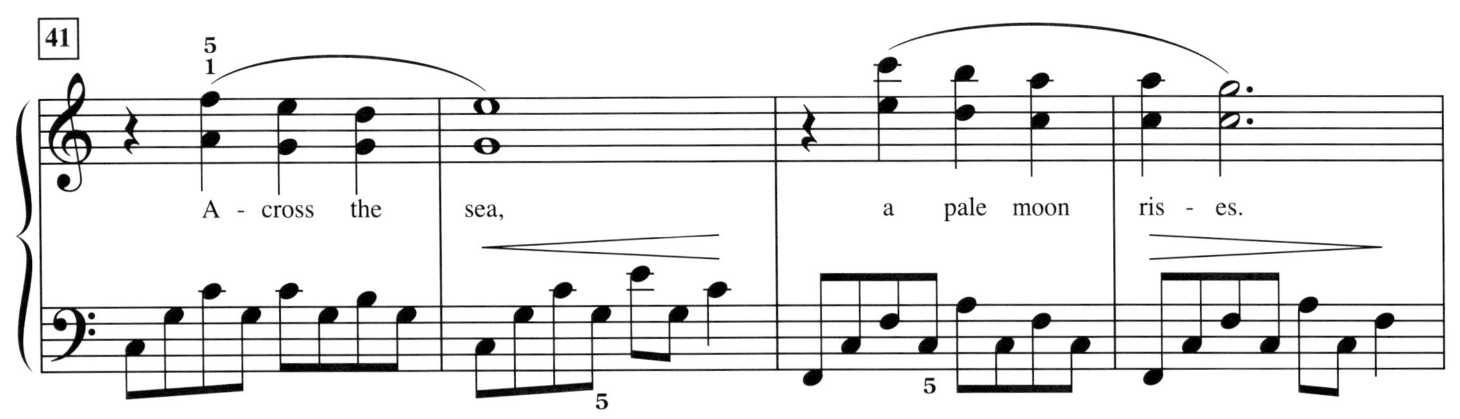
41
A - cross the sea, a pale moon ris - es.

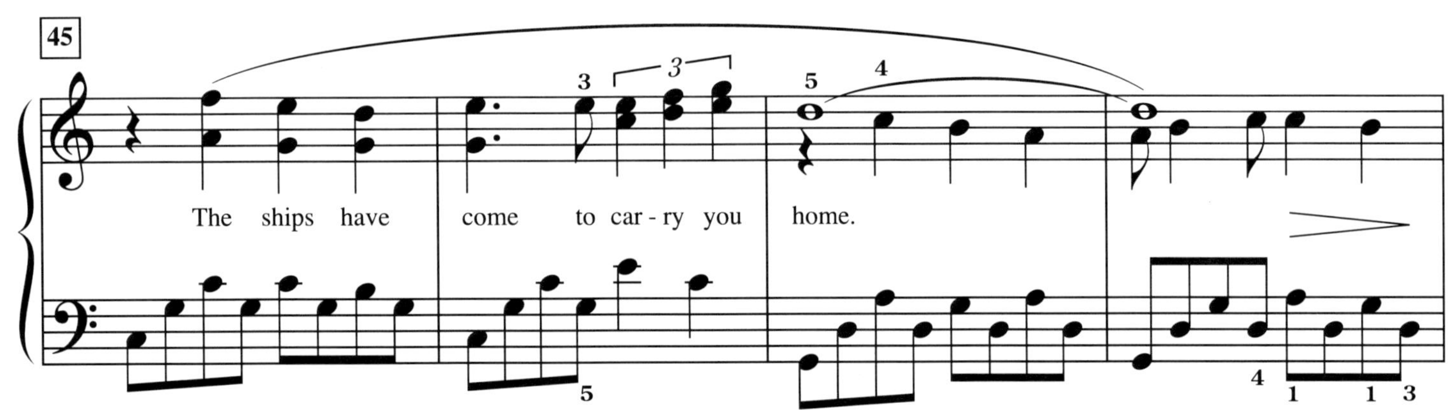
45
The ships have come to car - ry you home.

49
mf
And all will turn to sil - ver glass.

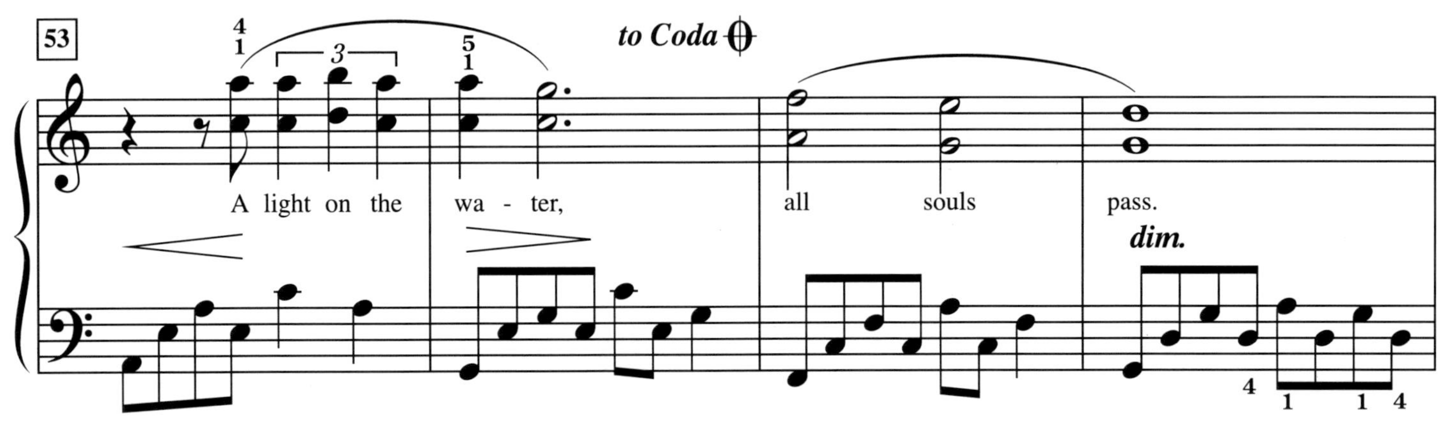
53
to Coda
A light on the wa - ter, all souls pass.
dim.

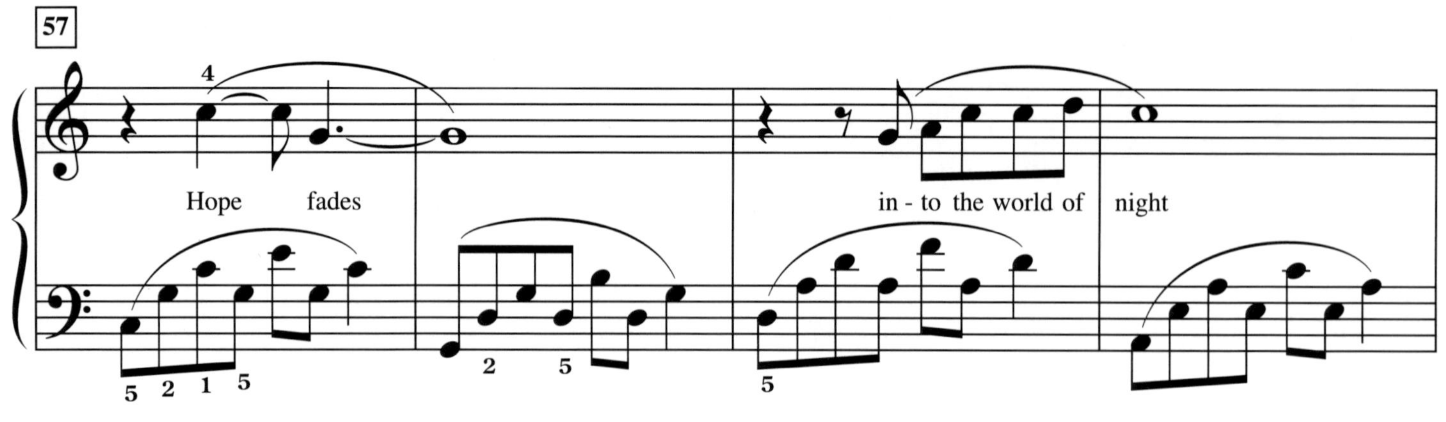
57
Hope   fades
in - to the world of   night

61
sim.
through shad - ows   fall - ing
out of mem - o - ry and

64
time.
mf
Don't   say

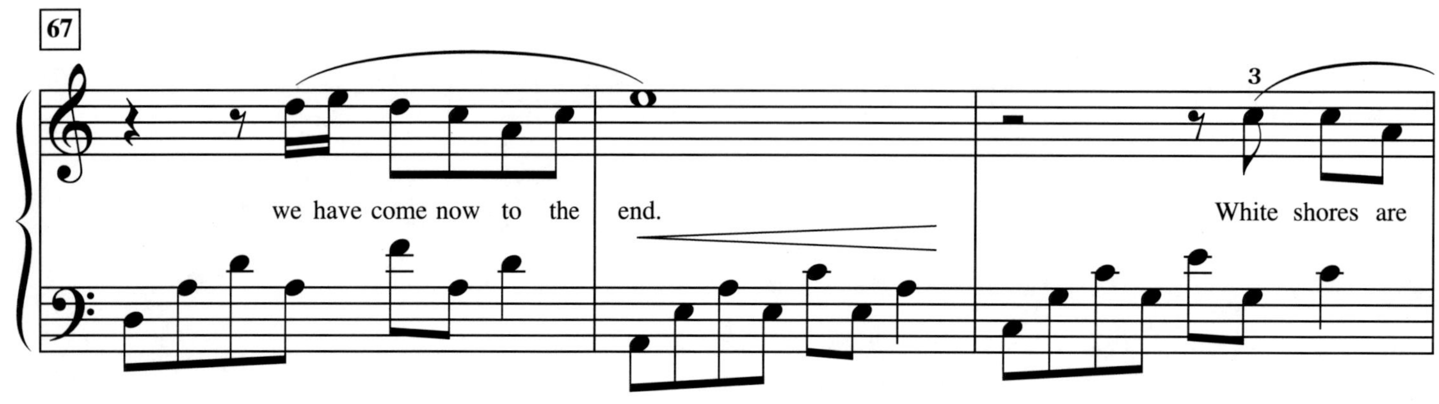
67
we have come now to the   end.
White shores are

70
1 2   1
call - ing.   You and I will meet a - gain.   And you'll be

73
D.S. al Coda
here   in my arms   cresc.   just   sleep - ing.
2 5

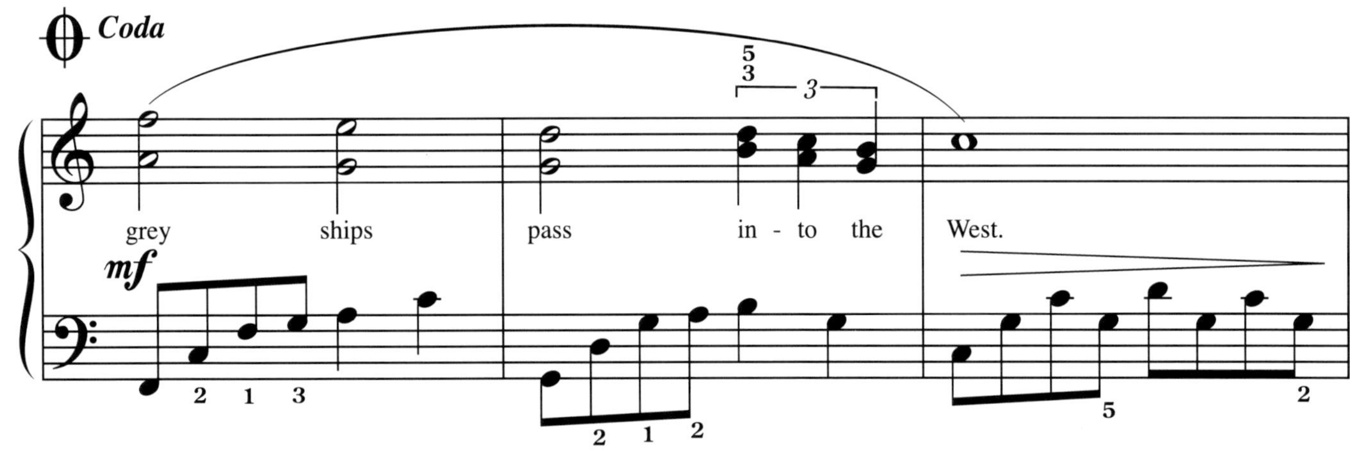
Coda
5
3   3
grey   ships   pass   in - to the   West.
mf
2 1 3   2 1 2   5   2

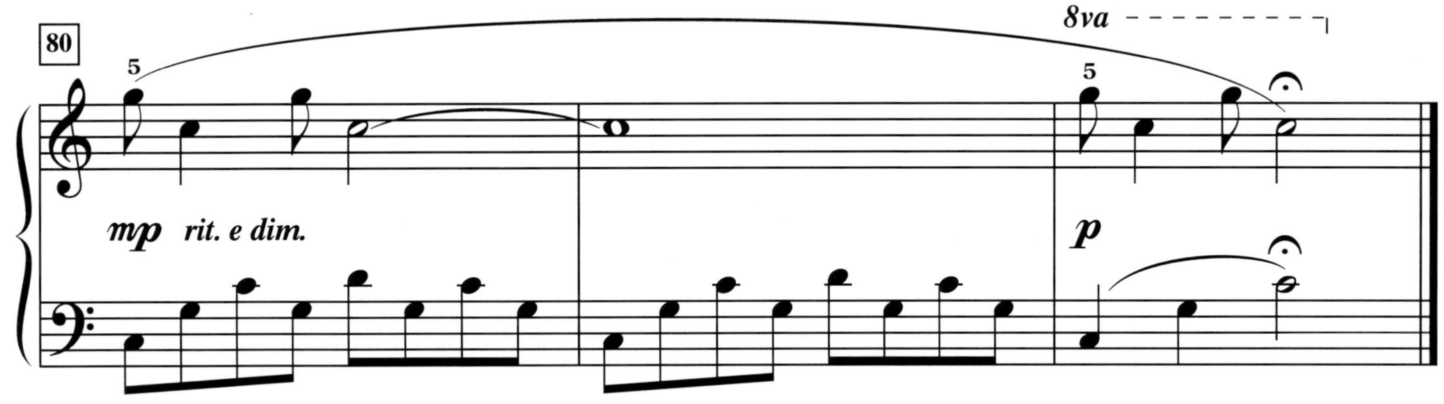
80
5
8va
5
mp rit. e dim.   p

A WHOLE NEW WORLD

Aladdin

Words by Tim Rice
Music by Alan Menken
Arranged by Dan Coates

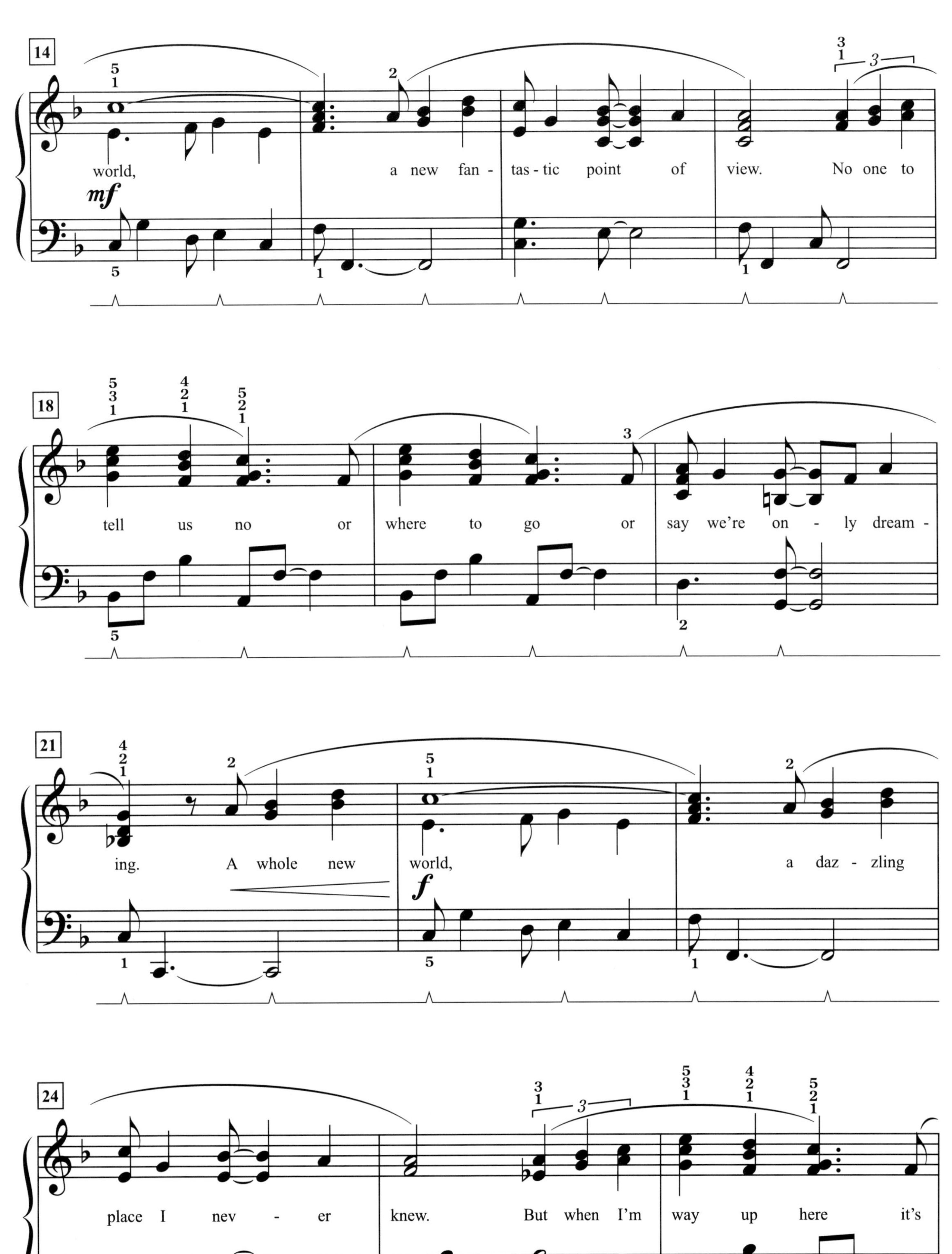
14
mf
world,
a new fan - tas - tic point of view. No one to
18
tell us no or where to go or say we're on - ly dream -
21
f
ing. A whole new world,
a daz - zling
24
place I nev - er knew. But when I'm way up here it's

27
cry - stal clear that now I'm in a whole new world with you.
mf

31
A whole new world, that's where we'll

34
be. A thrill - ing chase, a won - d'rous

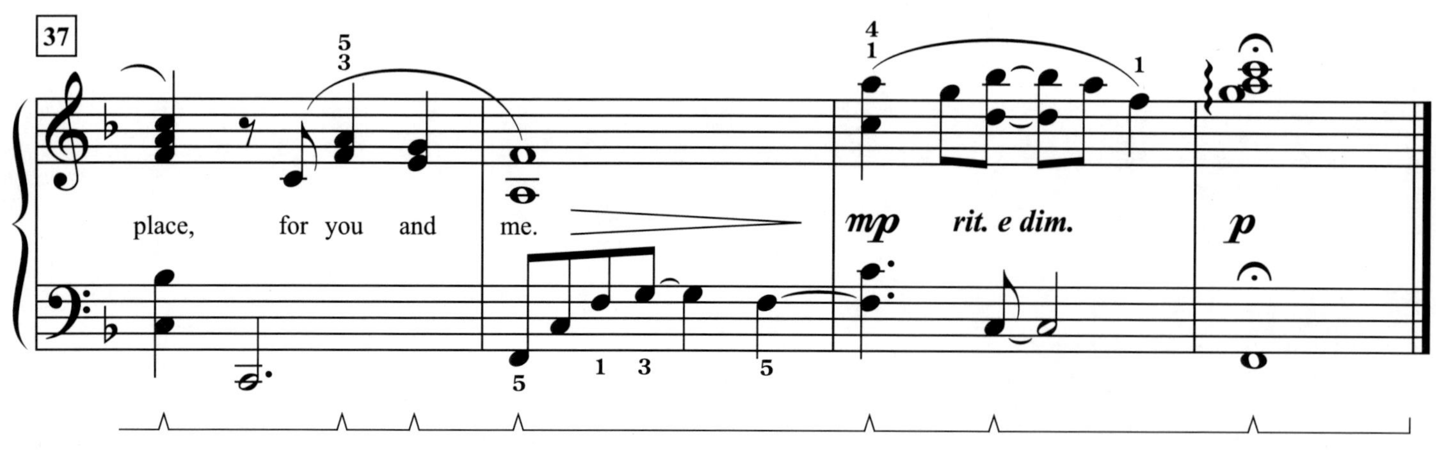
37
place, for you and me. mp rit. e dim. p

THE PINK PANTHER

The Pink Panther

By Henry Mancini
Arranged by Dan Coates

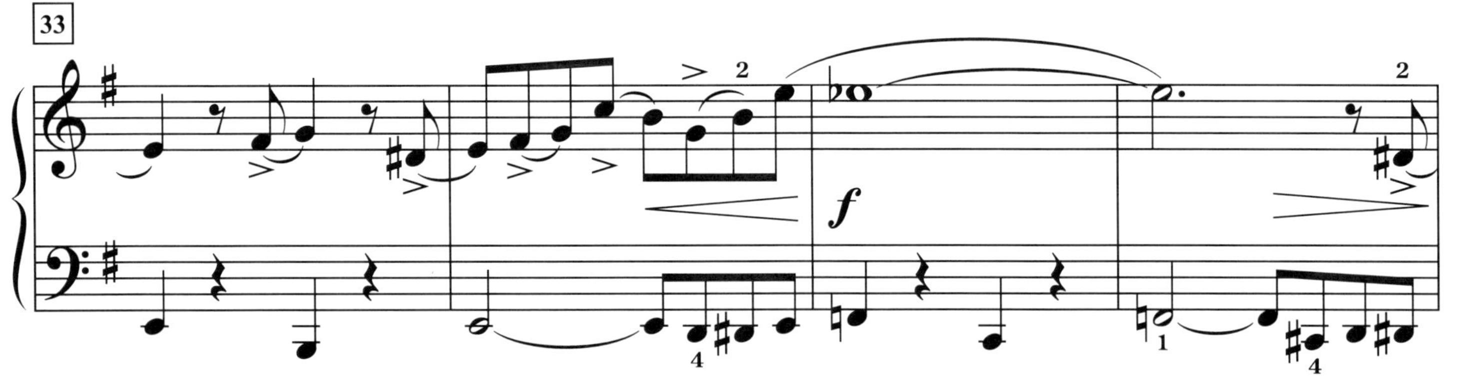

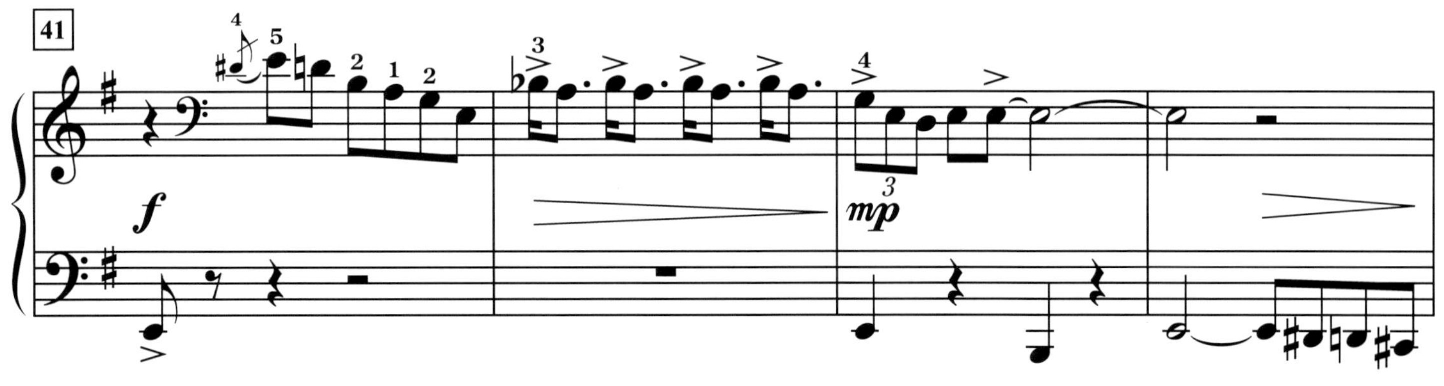